LO-PAN

In Tensions
ALR014

Published by

Aqualamb

LO-PAN:
Skot Thompson – Bass
Jeff Martin – Vocals
Chris Thompson – Guitar
Jesse Bartz – Drums

Dumb Asphalt (Ass Fault) Tour diary written by:
Jesse Bartz and Skot Thompson

Artwork:
Chris Smith: 7, 11-19, 28-29, 52
Jason Alexander Byers: 31, 53
Alexander von Weiding: 55
Brian Ewing, Becky Cloonan: 76
Ronnie Miller: 77
Joe Fortunato: 79
Skot Thompson: 81

Photography:
Dan Roll: 4, 20
Jesse Bartz: 22, 26, 46, 74, 98
Dan Gillies: 45
Meghan Ralston: 68
Paul Cunningham: 92
Jeff Martin: 102

All Songs written by LO-PAN
© LO-PAN All Rights Reserved
All lyrics written by Jeff Martin and reprinted by permission

First Printing: Edition of 500
ISBN: 978-0-9985211-0-7

aqualamb.org / lopandemic.com

CONTENTS

In Tensions 6
Colossus 30
Salvador 54
Sasquanaut 78

The music for *In Tensions*
can be downloaded
via the link below:

http://aqualamb.org/014

Lo-Pan Is: (L-R) Skot Thompson – Bass, Jeff Martin – Vocals, Chris Thompson – Guitar, Jesse Bartz – Drums

LO-PAN / *In Tensions* / JANUARY 13, 2017

LO-PAN / *In Tensions* / JANUARY 13, 2017

1. GO WEST
2. SINK OR SWIM
3. LONG LIVE THE KING
4. ALEXIS
5. PATHFINDER

SKOT THOMPSON – BASS
JEFF MARTIN – VOCALS
JESSE BARTZ – DRUMS
ADRIAN LEE ZAMBRANO – GUITAR

Produced by Lo-Pan
Recorded and Engineered by Joe Viers at Sonic Lounge
Songs 1-3 Mixed by Jonathan Nunez
Songs 4 & 5 Mixed by Ryan Haft
Mastered by Carl Saff at Saff Mastering
Art and Layout by Chris Smith at Grey Aria Design

All songs written and performed by Lo-Pan
© and ℗ Lo-Pan under exclusive license to Aqualamb Records (ASCAP)

GO WEST

Head west to a home beyond the deep
Black out the sun as you go
Take down your banners and be silent. Now.
Revise the vows that you've made. Yeah every word that you know.
Step heavy, for to live is bittersweet

Find nothing on the bloody shore
Overcome by the petulant sea

They say the west is a tomb
The wind clearing everything you've ever done
Take down your banners don't you let them see-you-cry
On this sacred ground. No.
Rest easy now your journey is complete

Find everything you wanted here
Overcome by cerulean sky… who said you can't go home

Time runs one way
Its strong its set
Its everyone you've ever known
Its everywhere you been

Find nothing on that bloody shore
Overcome by the petulant sea
I just wanna go home
Who says you cant go home?

Time runs one way
Its strong its set
Its everyone you've ever known
Its everywhere you been
I just wanna go home
Who says you cant go home?

Its everywhere you've been
Its everyone you've known
Unending bloody shore
Take down your banners – don't you let them see you cry

SINK OR SWIM

I turned away from you
You never knew – and its dangerous to perceive
I walk the streets that I knew
Sitting silent – and I'm begging for repreive

I'm drowning in you. Your words have weight for me
And I'm drowning in the deep
Been drifting in love – lets sail infinitely
Navigate the open sea
There was a time I lived for you
I knew the burden, and now I'm shouldering the cross
The pedestal I placed you on
Is high above me – in the golden age of loss

I'm drowning in you. Your words have weight for me
And I'm drowning in the deep.
We've suffered enough. Lets sail for calmer seas.
Ride the waves of bittersweet

Found my way – to the stage I'm standing on.
I romanticize the early days
I just can't seem to find the sun – the renewing one

Yes I found my way – to the open waves sustaining me
I criticize my later years
I just can't seem to find the sun – the precious one

LONG LIVE THE KING

I wake to remember
10 Years gone past
Adrift on the ocean
Light's fading fast –

I spent some time in the desert
I spent time in the shade
Spent time going over
The mistakes I made

I never thought I'd feel like a stranger
Don't think me insincere
I never thought you one to surrender
And after all these years – I'm

Lookin' for another sound – not another song
Not making any more excuses – it was always wrong

Overseeing his dominion
Sits the king on high
Win by attrition
Rule by tradition

Spent some time on the outside
That's the price I paid
It gave me time to consider
The mistakes I made
I never thought I'd feel like a stranger
Don't think me insincere
I never thought you one to surrender
And after all these years –
I want to make this clear
When all is said and done – you see me standing here
No I'm not running away from you
Let me make this clear
When its said and done – you see me standing here
You wont find me runnin' away from you

I tell myself to go
But my heart cant comply

Oh I cant walk away
And I still wonder why

Want to make this clear
When all is said and done – you see me standing here
No I'm not running away from you
Let me make this clear
When its said and done – you see me standing here
You wont find me runnin' away from you

Lookin' for another sound – not another song
Not making any more excuses – it was always wrong

ALEXIS

Your page, your light they've wasted away, for years
Just like the night when fading stars appear
All in the name of what? You find a name to despise and you give it up…
You gave yourself a name
All just to give it up. You're fed a line to repeat and you give it up…
You gave yourself away.
And late at night
Exposed to light
Your heart will stray

So how do you even live this way?
Face to face with the people you betray

It seems there's nothing left to say
Your page your light they're wasting away for years

And late at night
Exposed to light
You give yourself away

You give yourself away

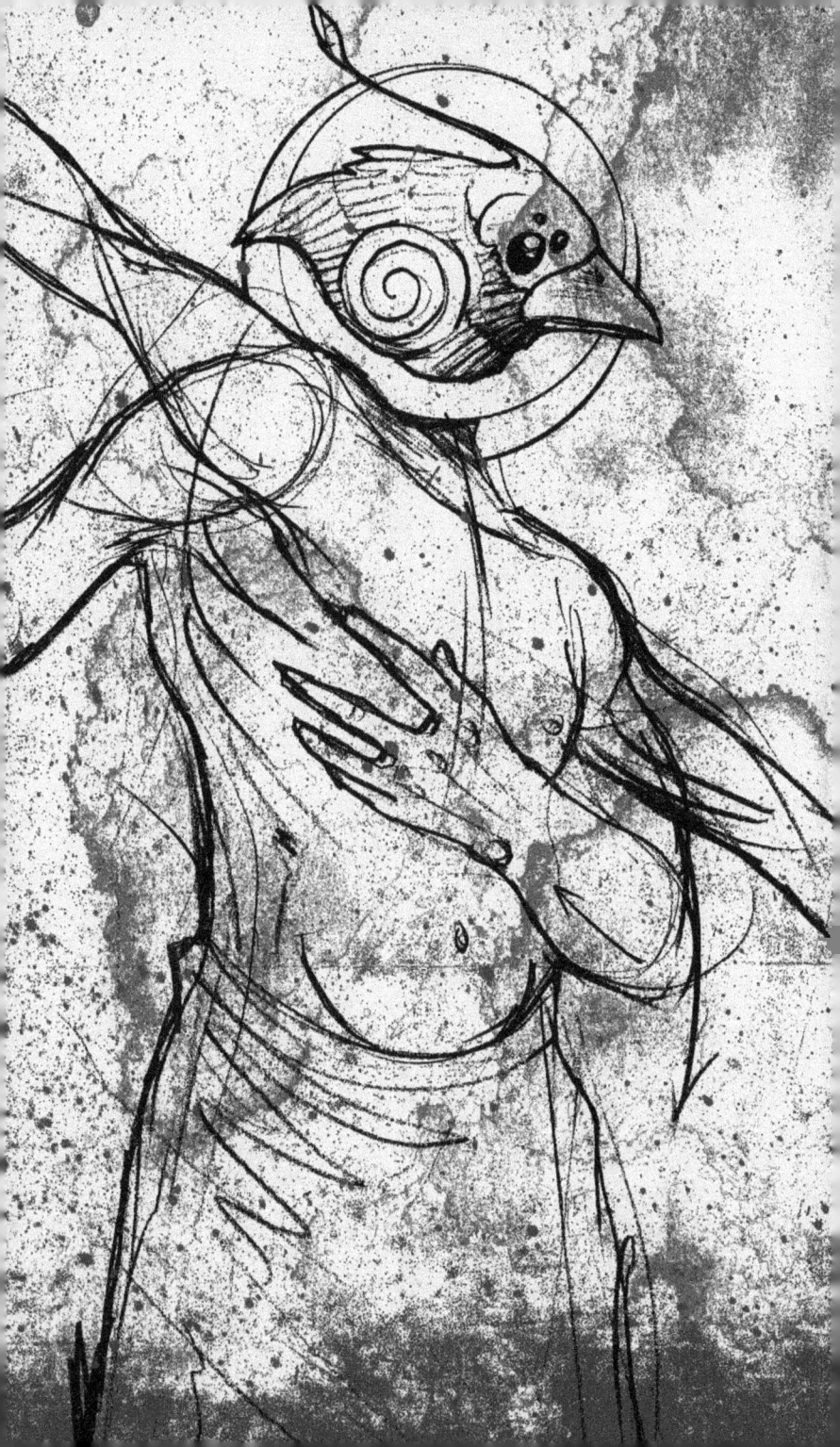

PATHFINDER

I see the weak ones rush into the storm
I need another way
Oh just another way to find my way

I hear the warlords bid us to conform
With every word they say
So quick to push you to your dying day
Talking in circles is the new art form
They need us to obey
I need another way to find my way

A higher elevation; new life form
I need another way
I need another way

I need a new way to ride…
And just one more summer. One more sun.
A new way not to live inside my head

I need a new way to see…
To see the long night through and the hard road done
Renewing all the things you thought you said

All those dead hot nights – but don't say a word
Don't say a word

All those long lonely miles – but don't say a word
No don't you say a word

I need a new way to ride…
And just one more summer. One more sun.
A new way not to live inside my head

I need a new way to see…
To see the long night through, the hard road done
Renewing all the things you thought you said

But here's to the end
I've seen the whole world over, the long road full
Still so much to see before I'm dead

I see the weak ones rush into the storm
I need another way
Talking in circles is the new art form
I need another way.
A higher elevation new life form
I need another way

I need another way
Show me another way

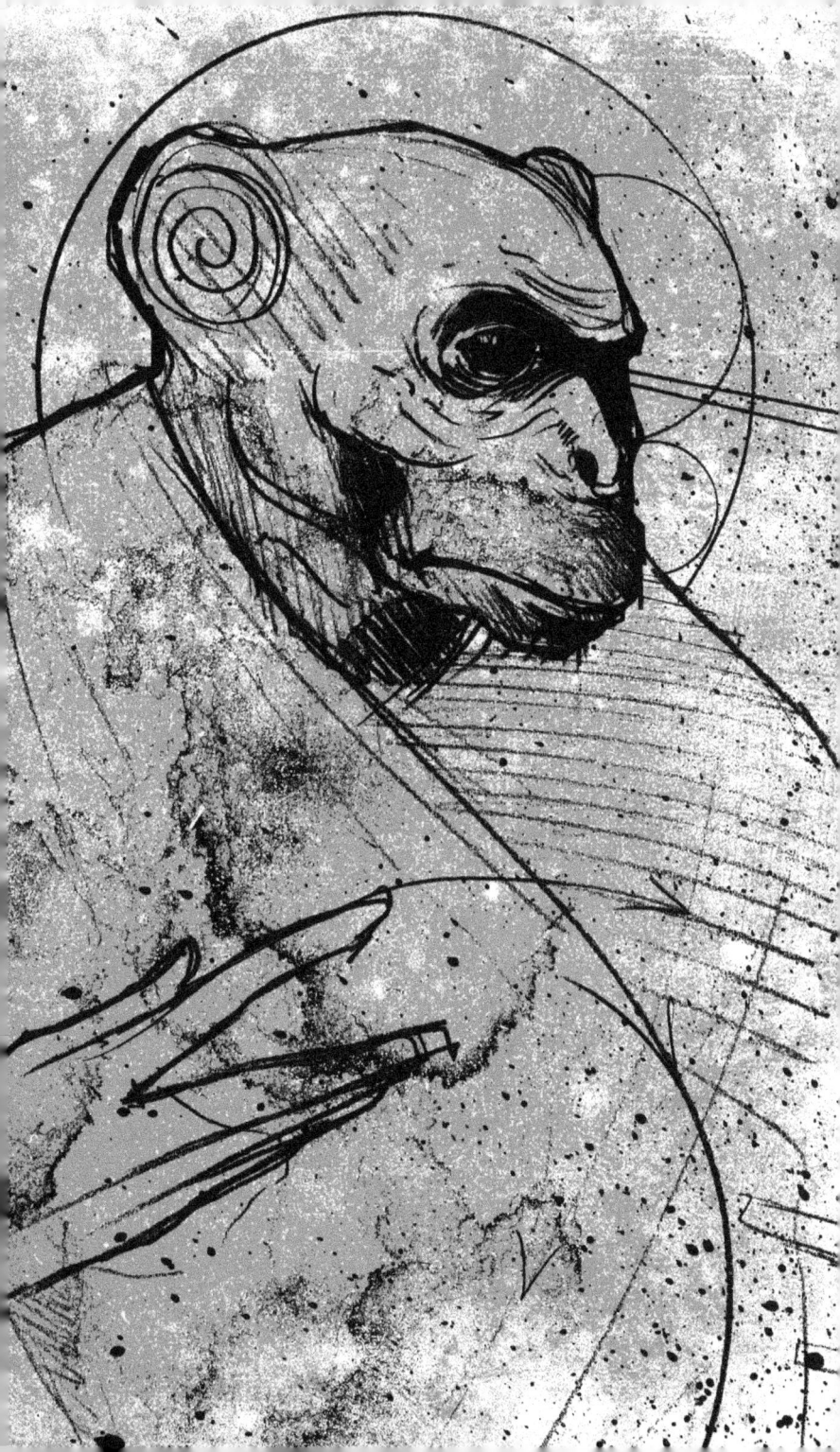

(L-R) Jesse Bartz – Drums, Skot Thompson – Bass, Adrian Lee Zambrano – Guitar, Jeff Martin – Vocals

8.19 Charlotte, NC   Milestone w/ ABW & Dirty Streets

Total shithole club in the best ways. We had a killer time and played great. This was Chris's 2nd show. Found a good place to crash after. All the bands played good tonight. The Seduction opened things up. Then Dirty Streets. Really like those guys. All in all for a first night of tour it was two thumbs.

8.21 NOLA   Siberia w/ ABW & Dirty Streets   HUMID

Great venue played here many times. The kitchen is top notch. We of course arrive way to early. First time we have ventured from the club at all. There was a driftwood pirate ship down the street and an art gallery that was celebrating the day of the dead. We played good tonight. Chris is really locking in. He is the one that motivated us to do a little exploring around. Lot's of positive vibes about him being a part of this now. Atomic Bitch Wax is a great band live and really good people as well. It has been like going to school every night watching them & the dirty streets dudes.

8.28 Psycho Vegas ~~Vegas~~ Hard Rock Hotel Vegas – too many other bands to list. Incredible day all around. We drove through the night to ~~get~~ arrive early. Got our equipment loaded in and got checked into our rooms to try and get a little sleep. The bands I will be seeing today: Fu Manchu, ASG, Baroness, Valkyrie, Sleep, Witch Mountain, Saviors, Mars Red Sky, and Fireball Ministry ~~...~~. I was also going to see Midnight but the line was way to long. ASG, Saviors, and Valkyrie were easily my favorites of the day. Great festival and venue. The stage we played was running about an hour behind and you could tell the stage hands and sound ~~engineers~~ engineer were all stressed and not having much fun by 10 pm sunday of a 3 day event. Note to self we will NEVER use any provided festival backline or sound engineer again. Just not fair to anyone involved. The artist suffers from playing unfamiliar equip & the audience suffers because the band isn't comfortable. Beyond that we played good and had a great time getting to hang with so many of our friends in one place. Good to also see so many people from other countries attend.

Chris's first tour has come to an end. He seems very happy. He is playing really well. Seems to be getting more locked in every performance. Looking forward to many more miles. And writing a lot more together.

Chevy Express, April 2016

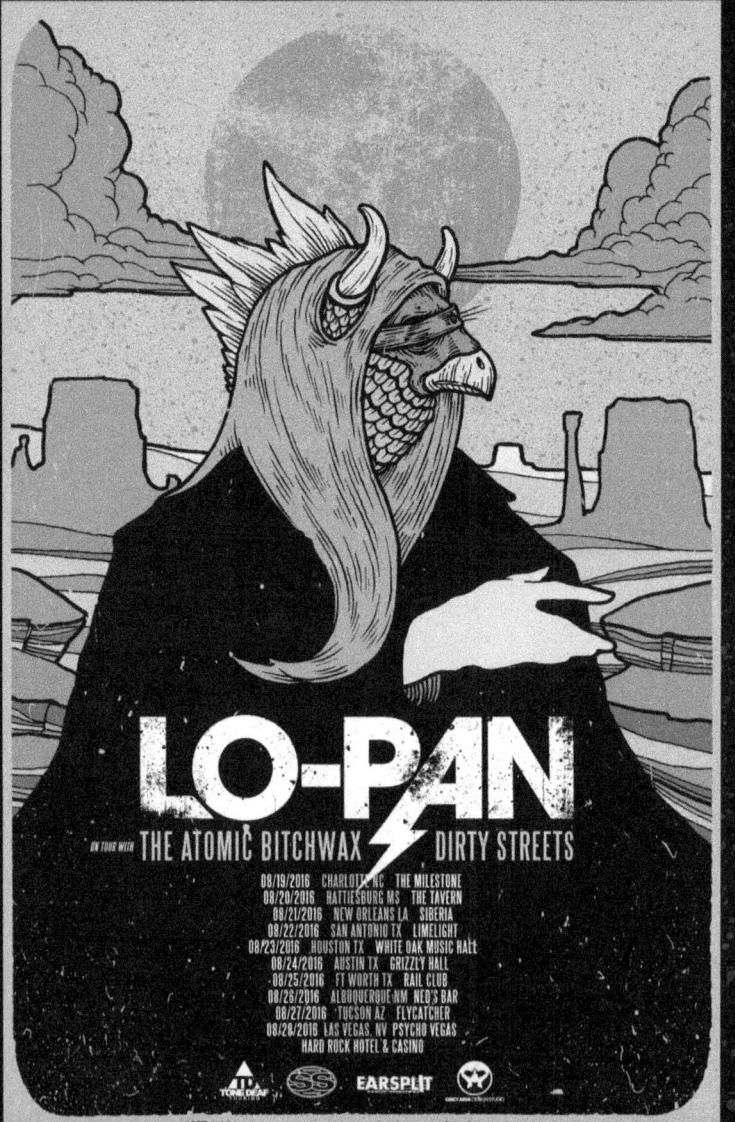

KEN mode
LO-PAN
OCT 28 COLUMBUS OH ACE OF CUPS
OCT 29 INDIANAPOLIS IN JOYFUL NOISE
OCT 30 COLUMBIA MO CAFE BERLIN
OCT 31 ST LOUIS MO THE DEMO
NOV 01 CHICAGO IL COBRA LOUNGE
NOV 02 DUBUQUE IA THE LIFT
NOV 03 MILWAUKEE WI THE CACTUS CLUB
NOV 04 MADISON WI DRAGON FLY LOUNGE
NOV 05 SIOUX FALLS SD TOTAL DRAG
NOV 06 MINNEAPOLIS MN HEXAGON BAR
Season of Mist
EARSPLIT
SEASONOFMIST.COM // SMALLSTONE.COM // EARSPLITCOMPOUND.COM

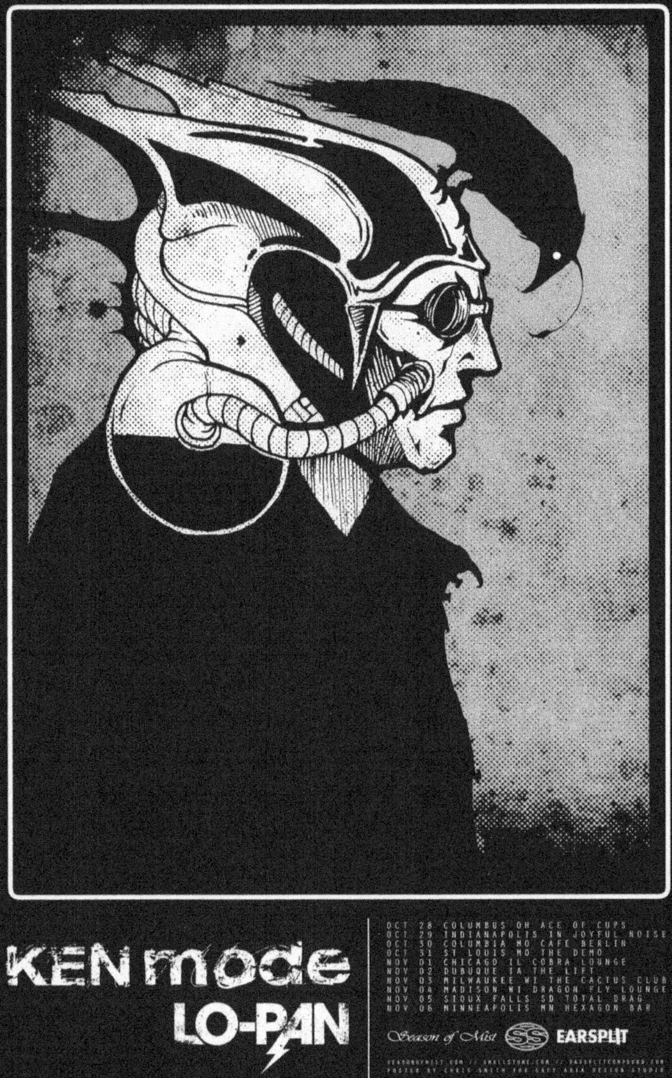

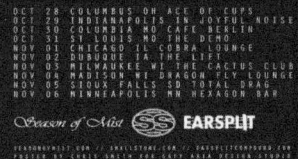

LO-PAN / *Colossus* / OCTOBER 7, 2014

LO-PAN / *Colossus* / OCTOBER 7, 2014

1. REGULUS
2. LAND OF THE BLIND
3. BLACK TOP REVELATION
4. MARATHON MAN
5. N.P.D.
6. COLOSSUS
7. VOX
8. EASTERN SEAS
9. RELO
10. THE DUKE

SKOT THOMPSON – BASS
JEFF MARTIN – VOCALS
JESSE BARTZ – DRUMS
BRIAN FRISTOE – GUITAR

Additional Vocals by Jason Alexander Byers on "Vox"
All Songs Written and Performed by Lo-Pan
SS-152 (Small Stone Records) 2014
Produced by Andrew Schneider and Lo-Pan
Engineered and Mixed by Andrew Schneider
Recorded at Translator Audio Brooklyn, NY
Mastered by Carl Saff at Saff Mastering
Art by Jason Alexander Byers
Layout by Johnathan Swafford

REGULUS

The old and sweet take over homeland's tomorrow
And onward goes the time — we save all
And inward go the years — I say no
And blinded from the light of the sun
Still moving — souvenirs we hold none

So long

And onward goes the time of our lives
And inward comes the flood by which you thrive
Still blinded by the light of the sun
Still moving — souvenirs we hold none
Those sold in street have taken a page from the new soul

So long

Still half way to the sun
Half way to the sun
You're not the only one
The reckoning's begun

Everything's undone
You're not the only one

The old and sweet take over homeland's tomorrow

Those sold in street have taken a page from the new soul

And onward goes the time of our lives
And inward comes the flood by which you thrive
Still blinded from the light of the sun

LAND OF THE BLIND

Burn the book that you've been sold – fill up the sky
Create new from all things old – time is nigh
Straighten all that which you fold – times on your side

Below

Journey from oblivions fall – on the rise
Living with decisions maze – close your eyes
Measure the ascent of time – claim your prize
Below

One eye open – one eye closed to see the kingdom of the light prevail
Kingdom of many, kingdom of one will see dominion of the dark fail

Fill up the sky with the fire on high – throw the pages on the bonfire
For you and I the time is nigh – feel the heat of the rolling pyre

Throw the pages on the bonfire
Throw the pages on the fire

One eye open – one eye closed – to see the kingdom of the light prevail
Kingdom of many – kingdom of one – will see dominion of the dark fail
Throw the pages on the bonfire
Throw the pages on the fire

BLACK TOP REVELATION

Found sacrifice on a black top highway
Dressed all in white and singing songs of love
I laid a message down on the blessed alter
One hundred twenty degrees in the burning sun
I read the minds of the willing in a revelation
Four hundred thousand to the wailing wall
I tore out the throat of the voice of reason
Sound the angels trumpets to destroy us all

What you been readin'
Is declared to be
Malicious in nature
Sounds like a heresy

I found the ashes of the phoenix on the highest mountain
Saw the reddest of sunsets in the devils eye
I've been high enough to call it planetary
Saw the kingdom of shadows on a moonless night
I've been cheated and followed into conflagration
Still the biggest lover and the biggest liar
I've been faded and intimated elevation
I've see the dragon coming for me, breathing fire.

MARATHON MAN

I'm waking up to a brave new world now – on the dark side of the street
The blood diamonds are shining bright now – on everyone you meet

The putrid stench of sinning
No time i'm busy winning
This is just the beginning
The earth will still be spinning

The deck is stacked against you – it's time to take a stand
Embrace the dark side of you – rise up and make demands
Steal some steal big steal a little – take everything you can

The herd is culled by thinning
The status quo unpinning
This is just the beginning
The earth will still be spinning round

Just for you – heading for you – get up and fly away
More for you – to abhor you – hear every word they say
Just for you – all just for you – get up and fly away
More for you – to abhor you – but you ain't got much to say

Unredeemed in the name of the father
You never saw what you wanted to see
You're stuck underwater breathing
Said you're in jail but you're holding the key
Yeah there's no good or bad, just best now
To see who's left at the end of the mile
Just to push on through and hold that grip
You'll be the one at the top of the pile

Just for you – heading for you – get up and fly away
More for you – to abhor you – hear every word they say
Just for you – all just for you – get up and fly away
More for you – to abhor you – but you ain't got much to say

Unredeemed in the name of the father
You never saw what you wanted to see
Yeah you're stuck underwater breathing
Said you're in jail but you're holding the key
Yeah there's no good or bad, just best now
To see who's left at the end of the mile
Just to push on through and hold that grip
You'll be the one at the top of the pile

For you – heading for you – you're running away – you're running away!
For you – straight for you – you're running away – you're running away!
You're running away – you're running away – you're running away!
For you – more for you – you're running away – you're running away!
More you – to abhor you – you're running away – you're running away!

I'm waking up to a brave new world now – on the dark side of the street
The blood diamonds are shining bright now – on everyone you meet

The putrid stench of sinning
No time I'm busy winning
This is just the beginning
The earth will still be spinning

For you – heading for you – you're running away – you're running away!
For you – straight for you – you're running away – you're running away!

N.P.D.

The face of pride
Has 50 eyes
Cut off the head the beast survives

Then out the mouth comes a different story.
Feeling better — but looking like the enemy
And underneath there's a sinister embrace
Beyond redemption — I perpetrate repeatedly

The face of pride
Is slow to die
Shameless and fleeting

And in the heart, where desire breeds
I'm boiling over, I form my own reality
And all the while there's the walls I've put in place

I'm not sorry.
No I don't regret a thing.

How many does it take?
To feel alive?
To feel satisfied?
To feel satisfied?

The beast survives
The face survives

COLOSSUS

Rolling backwards, slowly stepping on a way of life denied
Feeling better – learning something is the way to win
Find the center, empty pockets are a good place to begin
It feels better to found out for yourself

You'll find no solace living your religious life of sin
You can't cleanse it – the rivers won't wash it way
You'll find no answers sitting home and waiting to begin
So take cover – you know you can't save 'em all

Rolling backwards, holding onto something that resembles piece of mind
Getting better – building something is the way to win
I'm not bitter – the mediocre are the first ones to ascend
It feels better to find out for yourself

You'll find no solace living your religious life of sin
You can't cleanse it – the rivers won't wash it way
You'll find no answers sitting home and waiting to begin
So take cover – you know you can't save 'em all

You'll find no answers living a religious life, my friend
You can't cleanse it- the rivers won't wash it away
You'll find no solace wishing on the spirits of dead men
So take cover – you know you can't save 'em all

Said living is the only way to find
To walk it is the only way to find

What you need
You're on your own

It's easy to deny it
To take it on

Colossus on your feet
You are sure to meet
Your piece of mind

VOX

Never thought I'd be a sure shot, still I portend
Giving nothing to the front side – breaks or it bends
When I need a new forgiveness – I start from within

Oh I still believe in dark voices

I have desire to be upended – I summon the wind
Still I'm tethered to the half-light – seems such a sin
And when I need to feel the old ways – I start from within

Oh I till heed those dark voices

Dark words to call on the breeze
To shake the ground and stir the trees
Dark prophesies to see it bent
Translate the message that the old ones sent

So choose well, words you speak – words to carry – words to save you
On wings – words must fly – words to steady – words to bind you

So choose well, words you speak – words to carry – words to save you
On wings – words must fly – words to steady – words to guide you

EASTERN SEAS

Oh fair haired, enchanting one – hear me
I'm bleeding on a moonless ocean night and I'm heeding your call so I don't fade away
Left on a dream so long ago – do you see me?
I'm fading away
Oh green eyes of the eastern seas – free me
Where I go you cannot go and I won't be back again.
The deep holds the secrets of the dead – can you feel me?
I'm reaching out

Oh lighthouse of the endless waves – find me
Torn between the darkness and the light and i'm hoping to blindly find the other shore
Oh goddess of the sailor moon – guide me
Please hold out your hand
Oh vagabond of divided hearts – is me
Caught between the darkness and the light – and time's no friend of mine
Oh fair haired enchanting one – find me
I'm fading – fading away
Drifting and falling through triumph and trial alike
Greeted by darkness surprising, devoid of light
Sailing seas blindly – darkness a bitter fight
Sea winds grow colder – prolonging the endless night
Are you calling? Are you calling out to me?
I'm sailing and I'm never coming home.
Your memory's fading – can't find your face again
Fair haired traveler guide me home to
Embrace your memory
Straight on 'til morning

RELO

Silent, contented. To see the other half move.
Eyes on the static — the iteration removed

I'm pleased to be leaving what's been sitting on the other floor
I let it stand it my way until I unlock the door.

Transforming — I'm on another wave
I go it alone — another life I save.

Soiled confinement into the waking man's tomb.
Haze of restriction — another life form removed

I'm pleased to be leaving what's been sitting on the other shore
I let it stand it my way until I unlock the door.

Transforming — I'm on another wave
I go it alone — another life I save.

I'm pulling it together to go the opposite way.
Leaving yet another — receiving light from a better day

THE DUKE

Snidely tossing out — all those who come to see
Howling for the moon to return to sea
Bowing out from one out to three

Ever downward
What it means to find the other/another one

Breathe deeper
Arching towards the sun

Bring water
Never knowing what your limits are

Bleed farther
Open eyes and...
Said nothing of the cost in this dangerous game you play
When I die, it'll all be great, paint a picture of the grey
Held down in an open field, never hope get away
Bringing faithful to the countryside hoping to their fears allay

Memory which descends — under fates decree
Rushing to defend — that which weighs on me
Holding to the line — nothing sanct or free

A game to play

(L-R) Brian Fristoe— Guitar, Jeff Martin — Vocals, Skot Thompson — Bass, Jesse Bartz — Drums

Junction View, May 2013

8.29 Albuquerque, NM - Sister
Great Venue, Great Staff. Long drive back across the desert today. ~~This place was the~~ Good show all around. Trying to setup some European stuff for early 2015. Not the easiest thing to do while on the road. Another drive across the desert tomorrow. Fuck my cymbals. American Flag bandannas for life. College football starts tomorrow and I am happy the off season is over. Probably going to concentrate a lot on football this year since I am on the road and have lots of time.

8.30 Oklahoma City, OK - The Conservatory
What a dump! I kind of like it. shitty gravel parking ~~lot~~ We have played here a lot of times. Great staff and crowd. We do well here. The kids always seem to support us. Jeff & Skot got a room for the night. Some hotel that had tons of dealers and prostitutes working out of it. Brian & I took the van and I could barely sleep because of the parking lot.

8.31 Dallas - ~~Doublewide~~
Awesome double room venue with a courtyard. Great staff good crowd. easy parking and load in. Got there WAY too early so ~~we~~ skot and I went walking around deep elm. Pretty cool area. Kyle from Mothership showed up tonight. Great to hang with him. I got a couple of new crash cymbals today. The set is sounding very strong for this tour.

9.12 Richmond, VA - Strange Matter.
We of course arrive way to early for any reasonable human. But I killed time walking around the campus there. This day marked the first time Jeff, Skot, and I did laundry at a laundrymat while on the road. Brian was pre-occupied with getting juice for his vapor pen. Played well! Good crowd great PA and great staff.

9.13 Baltimore, MD   Metro Gallery
We went early and got some crabs from the inner harbor. Really cool venue great sound

LO-PAN
ON TOUR THIS FALL WITH
black cobra

COLOSSUS
ALBUM AVAILABLE
10.07.14

08.28 PHOENIX, AZ	09.06 TAMPA, FL	09.14 PROVIDENCE, RI	09.23 CHICAGO, IL
08.29 ALBUQUERQUE, NM	09.07 MIAMI, FL	09.15 BURLINGTON, VT	09.24 MINNEAPOLIS, MN
08.30 OKLAHOMA CITY, OK	09.08 ORLANDO, FL	09.16 BOSTON, MA	09.26 LAWRENCE, KS
08.31 DALLAS, TX	09.09 ATLANTA, GA	09.17 PHILADELPHIA, PA	09.27 DENVER, CO
09.02 AUSTIN, TX	09.10 ASHEVILLE, NC	09.18 NEW YORK, NY	09.28 SALT LAKE CITY, UT
09.03 HOUSTON, TX	09.11 CHARLOTTE, NC	09.19 SYRACUSE, NY	09.29 LAS VEGAS, NV
09.04 NEW ORLEANS, LA	09.12 RICHMOND, VA	09.20 ROCHESTER, NY	10.01 VENTURA, CA
09.05 PENSACOLA, FL	09.13 WASHINGTON DC	09.22 PITTSBURGH, PA	10.02 OAKLAND, CA

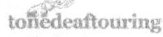
tonedeaftouring
tonedeaftouring.com

smallstone.com

EARSPLIT
earsplitcompound.com

LO-PAN / *Salvador* / MAY 24, 2011

LO-PAN / *Salvador* / MAY 24, 2011

1. EL DORADO
2. BLEEDING OUT
3. SEED
4. BIRD OF PREY
5. DECIDUOUS
6. INTRO
7. CHICHEN ITZA
8. SPARTACUS
9. STRUCK MATCH
10. GENERATIONS
11. SOLO

SKOT THOMPSON — BASS
JEFF MARTIN — VOCALS
JESSE BARTZ — DRUMS
BRIAN FRISTOE — GUITAR

All songs written and performed by Lo-Pan
SS-116 (Small Stone Records) 2011
Produced, Recorded, and Mixed by Benny Grotto at Mad Oak Studios Allston, MA
Mastered by Chris Goosman at Baseline Audio Labs Ann Arbor, MI
Album Artwork by Alexander von Weiding

EL DORADO

Sleep

Whisper – not to me – o death with wings adorned in grace
Over the mountains of the moon

Seated – figure perched on shrines which bode eternal rest
Wasted – pilgrims shadow speaks in earthly tongue to test
Over the mountains moon

Adorned in grace

Vibrant yet fell so very soon

Over the mountains
Over the mountains of the moon

Pilgrims shadow speaks to test
Death in shadow – perched on shrines – boding eternal rest

Whisper not to me – o death

BLEEDING OUT

My truth is evident
Burning high with the flames of discontent
My opportunities all came and went
I'm screaming "yes" to policies of modern day dissent
I'm feeling high from lack of oxygen
Like minus 3 on a scale from one to ten
I know I'm dying but don't know when
I'm bleeding out just a case of paper to pen

Bleeding out the only way to keep me sane let it out the only thing that feels humane it don't work – it don't work so keep bleeding

My lie is obvious falling short of poetic its odious exaggeration can be copious falling blind can become disastrous
Blood loss is black as sin recalling all the horrid things I've taken in throw it out and pull the pin bleeding out but my blood is running thin

And when the bleeding is over – it's over – there's nothing left to say and when the digging inside is over – so over – it's just a bill to pay and when the building is under – from under – I do it the same way

Building and steaming, opened and bleeding, written and freed from inside

SEED

Buried under a capital tuesday find
I'm imprisoned by lights that won't shine
Things that held me down I have sold
Hidden phrases a measure too bold
What is lying and who is for true
Violent winter surrounding you – so I say
White noise bleeding into afternoon – programmed from 1 to 3
Vague and dusty is love unrefined – brown wrappers can't fill the need. No
New born babies come broken and blue – good rapists have scary needs. Yeah
Always bleeding but it's still fun to play – vastly sowing seeds

6 Rounds chambered and set to explode violent winter exploring you – so I say

Heaven sounding unwanted advice – stay on channel 3
Always running and left undefined – brown wrappers conceal the need. No
New born babies stay broken and blue – good rapists enjoy the need. Yeah
None worth loving but still fun to play – vastly sowing seeds

Untold numbers of shells on the floor violent seasons exposing you – so I say
Pin the tail – hold it down – pound it home sit in silent rage

This is how it feels when the blood keeps coming/when the blood keeps coming
Devouring pieces, devoured whole
The overseer is overseen
Knives are delicate and so serene

Things that held me down I have sold
Hidden phrases a measure too bold
What is lying and who is for true
Violent winter surrounding you so I say

Vastly sowing seeds

BIRD OF PREY

Rolling southward at midnight – one of the chosen few
Finding no words, so I sit tight – on a lovely mountain view
Moonlight flashing through windows – I'll never see again
Running loaded and silent – on a stale cool wind

Bloodshot eyes seeing nothing – but hearing everything
Willing distance and progress – and all the spoils that it brings
Wear defeat like a road sign – another tragic tale
Muddy greens – and a sea of blue to sail
Speeding northbound – degraded – more with each passing day
Light exposing each dollar – and every dream I throw away
Words repeated mean nothing – to me the least of all
Sound that drowns out all troubles – I hear the call.

Bringing blood to my ears – giving words to my tears caller holding the line – raw allegiance confines

Recycled half dead memories – I play them all again it brings a smile to my face playing games I was never supposed to win "red letter days" is the melody – to keep the walls in place reliving nights made of amber lights – a sea of heads to keep the pace

Prevailing winds carry off again – a great and terrible sound a living breathing pulsing noise – causing foot to meet the ground red letter days cause soliloquy – a sieve from brain to voice retrieving lies seen through rosy eyes – believing soon becomes a choice

Rolling southward at midnight – one of the chosen few
Finding no words, so I sit tight – on a lovely mountain view
Words repeated mean nothing – to me the least of all
Sound that drowns out all troubles – I hear the call

With muddy greens and a sea of blue to sail

DECIDUOUS

Seed –turns to lidless canopy
I – lost – the forest for the trees
Vast – blue – a drop upon the endless sea
Dark – lush – and overwhelming me space – breeds – a harsh uncertainty

Blind and in the trees with a willingness to bleed
A harsh and jealous sea gives lessons painfully
Crashing down on me with sight – gained – eventually

CHICHEN ITZA

Bright sunshine
The lights that blind – the lights that blind
With reverence to the land
Proud and brutal hand on ancestral sand

Given up to waves
Pressed and bonded slaves
Blue and gold to save
Destruction came one day

Bright sunshine
The lights that blind – the lights that blind
With reverence to the land
Proud and brutal hand on ancestral sand

Given up to waves
Pressed and bonded slaves
Blue and gold to save

Given up to night
Broken ship in sight
Living what was right
Destruction came one day

You found your voice to stay – the sign taken away
When it's written – it's written on your hand

You found your voice to thrive – a voice to stay alive
The proudest of an age

Destruction came one day

SPARTACUS

Happiness breeds out in a generation
Accomplishments fade
Weed out the willing – painful separation
Blood on the snow
Breeding remorseless unsated dedicated

Under boot I won't live
My whole life i'd rather give
On my knees is no way
There must be a faster way

Fire – to take it all back
Show them the crack of the whip is no longer enough
Blood – blood on the streets
Show them we feed on the slabs of the rawest and the reddest meat

Watching their heads role down the middle of main street
Such a beautiful sight
Rivers run red with the blood of the greedy
Ashes to dust
Breeding remorseless unsated – resolute now

Under boot I won't live
My whole life i'd rather give
On my knees is no way
There must be a faster way

Fire – to take it all back
Show them the crack of the whip is no longer enough
Blood – blood on the streets
Show them we feed on the slabs of the rawest and the reddest meat

I'd rather die than live under your thumb now
Can vitriol save me from the power mad?
Vitriol make me numb take it away

Fire to take it all back

Under boot I won't live
My whole life I would give
On my knees is no way

Vitriol take me away
Vitriol make me numb

STRUCK MATCH

Perpetuated through insidious lies
Waged inside a fire
It's tough to stay alive and moving sometimes
It's right down to the wire

I'm burning and losing a life
I see it go
I'm leaving the battle behind
My heart and soul

My part time miseries
Seems like a game that never made much sense to me
See, it's just a shame
And all my paranoid fantasies – I can't repress the cracks erupting violently
See, it's just a shame
Frequent reflection – if I could do it all again
I'd stand remorseful and guilty of most every sin
I'm breathing and falling away

I'm burning and losing a life
I see it go
I'm leaving the battle behind
My heart and soul
You watch it fall away

Perpetuated through insidious lies
Waged inside a fire
It's tough to stay alive and moving sometimes
It's right down to the wire

I'm burning and losing a life – I see it go.

GENERATIONS

Fifteen footsteps and I make the call – you never noticed me
Years gone by still waiting on a prideful fall – bracing others not gingerly

Strides in earnest made and always trying to bridge the two – seasons sliding by

Generations of a silence built from one degree
Choices made are clear for some to see
Flash resentments and issues passed from large to small
Handed down and passed to me.

Bloodlines crosses and...Cast aside and...Cut and tied again.
Voices heard then...Lost to time then...Treated with no urgency.
Bloodlines blurred and...Disregarded and...Ignored for a lifetime now.
Faces kissed then...Lost to blindness...Fool for a lifetime now.

Leaves left turn and fall...But the image remains –
Names have been stripped away – but the pictures remains
Once removed and dead inside – it fades in the sun
Blood still runs and the heart remains – a healing begun.

Healing begun – and the image remains. Healing's begun. But it still remains

Bloodlines crossed and cast aside and – cut and tied again
Voices heard then lost to time then treated with no urgency

I see your face

SOLO

Waiting on the rise and fall
Laid out before me like a mortal sin
Interrogated lies to all
Unending game that nobody wins

Taking it slow
So unsure just where to go
Dead set to realize
Nobody sees through another's eyes

Sacrificial lambs will rise
Is wisdom born out of the words you say
The grand canyon cut to size
Willing to see it in another way

Taking it slow
I'm so unsure just what I know
Dead set to realize
Nobody sees if nobody tries

Just let it go and watch it fade away

Just let it go and watch it fade away
Your word and bond will fall to ruin this way.

Just let it go
Or watch it fade away

Go solo

Cut down unsworn by sin
And never coming back again

Go solo

Brought down and cut to size
Can't see clear through another's eyes
Go solo

Go

(L-R) Jeff Martin – Vocals, Brian Fristoe– Guitar, Jesse Bartz – Drums, Skot Thompson – Bass

2012 West Coast Tour

6.17 Detroit, MI Corktown Tavern –
Stayed at Vince's (Year Of The Pig) printing studio. Slept well! Got a new Big Trouble In Little China shirt. Very good accomidations. Went and visited Hamilton (Smallstone) before leaving town. As always we slammed the Lafayette after the gig.

6.18 Chicago, Ill. Cobra Lounge –
Stayed at the venue. They have an upstairs apartment set up for touring bands. Over the top great place.

6.19 Madison, WI Club Inferno –

Stayed at the house of the band Dagger. Great accomidations. Very nice people. Arrived in town early and got lunch with our friend Brian Jensen (Capital City Tattoo). He took us to a place called Stalzy's. Unbelievably good food!! They named a sandwich for Lo-Pan. It consists of: double smoked brisket, double smoked bacon, swiss cheese, red onion, and spicy mustard served on house made light rye bread. –BAM–

Thur Nov 15 '12 - Emo's Austin, TX: First night of High On Fire, Goatwhore, Lo-Pan. Fairly long drive. Huge venue. Huge PA. We hurry up and wait and wait. Good to get there early and meet everyone. Long sound check but to be expected on first night. We played a solid set tonight. Short drive tomorrow. I am really feeling strong about this tour.

Fri. Nov 16 '12 - Korova San Antonio, TX: w/ HOF, Goatwhore, Venomous Maximus, HoD. Life changing experience at Smitty's in Lockhart, TX today. Our buddy Kenny from ATX said he knew the best BBQ in the world, he was right! No lie best in the world! Easy load in load out. Great venue. Seems like most of these venues will be stellar. I think we are driving back to ATX tonight. Love that town.

Sat Nov 17 '12 - Tree's Dallas, TX: w/ HOF, Goatwhore, Venomous Maximus. Another incredible venue. Really nice sound and stage. Got to change my bass strum head thanks to Kyle from Mothership. Good to see a lot of our friends coming out to these shows. Got our buddy Dan from Chapstik along for the whole tour. He has been a very welcomed addition to our equation. Things are running really smooth. We are playing strong sets. I am feeling really healthy. Easiest touring we have done yet. Almost to easy.

Ford Econoline E150, Summer 2011

BECKYCLOONAN.NET
BRIANEWING.COM
DECEMBER 5th • 2012
HIGH ON FIRE
GOATWHORE • LO-PAN
ACE OF CUPS • 2619 NORTH HIGH ST • COLUMBUS, OH 43202
HIGHONFIRE.NET

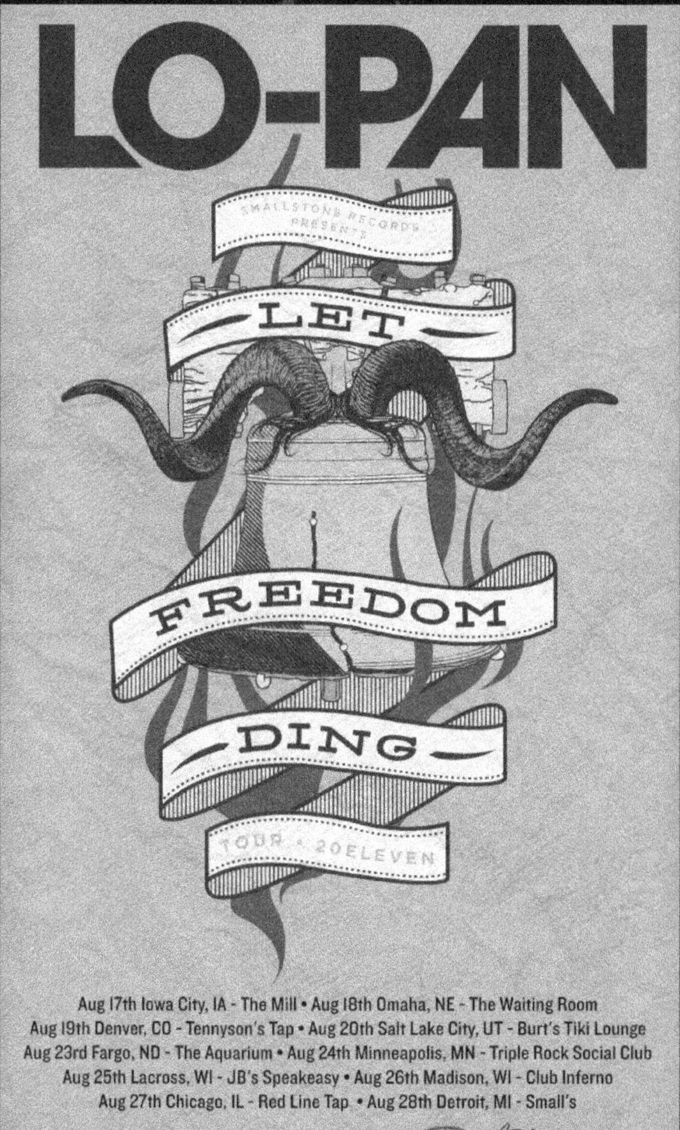
LO-PAN
SMALLSTONE RECORDS PRESENTS
LET
FREEDOM
DING
TOUR • 20ELEVEN
Aug 17th Iowa City, IA - The Mill • Aug 18th Omaha, NE - The Waiting Room
Aug 19th Denver, CO - Tennyson's Tap • Aug 20th Salt Lake City, UT - Burt's Tiki Lounge
Aug 23rd Fargo, ND - The Aquarium • Aug 24th Minneapolis, MN - Triple Rock Social Club
Aug 25th Lacross, WI - JB's Speakeasy • Aug 26th Madison, WI - Club Inferno
Aug 27th Chicago, IL - Red Line Tap • Aug 28th Detroit, MI - Small's
lopandemic.com • smallstone.com
Enfectious Erf

LO-PAN / *Sasquanaut* / JANUARY 25, 2011
(REMIXED & REMASTERED)

LO-PAN / *Sasquanaut* / 2006
(ORIGINAL PRESSING)

LO-PAN / *Sasquanaut* / JANUARY 25, 2011

1. DRAGLINE
2. SAVAGE HENRY
3. KURTZ
4. CALLAHAN
5. KRAMER
6. VEGA
7. VEGO
8. WADE GARRETT

SKOT THOMPSON – BASS
JEFF MARTIN – VOCALS
JESSE BARTZ – DRUMS
BRIAN FRISTOE – GUITAR

SS-110 (Small Stone Records) Repress 2010
Tracks 1-7:
Recorded and Engineered by Paul Maccarrone and "Buddy" Akita at Zombie Proof Studios
Cleveland, OH
Track 8:
Recorded and Engineered by Adam Smith at CDR Columbus, OH
Mixed by Benny Grotto at Mad Oak Studios Allston, MA
Mastered by Chris Goosman at Baseline Audio Labs Ann Arbor, MI
Artwork by Joe Fortunato at Blacklodge

LO-PAN / *Sasquanaut* / 2006

NLCD004 (Nice Life Records) Original 2008
Recorded and Engineered by Paul Maccarrone and "Buddy" Akita at Zombie Proof Studios
Cleveland, OH
Mixed by Paul Maccarrone and Lo-Pan
Mastered by Chris Goosman at Baseline Audio Labs Ann Arbor, MI
Cover Artwork by Skot Thompson
Inside Artwork by Jimbo Valentine at Amalgam Unlimited
Design Layout by Steve Janiak

DRAGLINE

Waiting on hard times – living a good time slow
the spell has me under – the spell that I'm under
waiting on good times – living on borrowed speed.
because I struggle I'm still fed – I struggle I'm still fed
Is boredom a cancer? I'm spotted and sold
are lyrics forgotten? I sure am – a measure too bold
concentrating on hard times – living a good time slow
the spell has me under – the spell that I'm under
waiting on hard times – living on borrowed speed.
because I struggle I'm still fed – I struggle I'm still fed
Is boredom a cancer? I'm spotted and sold
are lyrics forgotten? I sure am – as days slip away
is boredom a cancer? I'm spotted and sold
are lyrics forgotten? I sure am – a measure too bold
waiting on hard times – at the wall
wasn't there something about losing track of your mind?
Wasn't there something about losing sight of your head?
I swallow it down – and I drag it away

SAVAGE HENRY

Alone and driving – in the fast lane rushing to a criminals fate
Alive and flying – feeling insane in a tragedies wake
Alone and crying – feeling no pain rushing to my criminals fate
Awake and driving – drained in a tragedies wake
Do you settle nice and free? Dont you settle down? When will you take the open road to sea? Dont you settle down?
And have you given up on me? Persistance plants the seed
And if you bleed – then bleed for me dont give up on me
Do you see a need? Will you stop to feed?

KURTZ

Down – in my perverted grave
I've seen the horror of war and the genius of torture
Down all the masses and watch me kill pig after pig
Follow me down – to where the preacher saves
Where I've seen the acres of mindless invoke benediction –
Smile with their eyes closed – waiting for help that won't come – no it won't come
Ride them like slaves – this massacre saves
Long into night – I'll be feeding on plight
And sever the skies and feed on sad lies
You never left – you only disappeared
You never left – you only disappeared from day one
In summer days and summer nights
In shades of grey – in shades off white
You told the lie – it was a perfect last night
You told the lie a perfect view from down in my grave
Follow me down – in my perverted grave
Ive seen the genius of war – the horror of tortured
Down on the masses watch me land blow after blow
Ill ride em like slaves this massacre saves
Long into the night – I'll be feeding on plight
Sever the skies and feed on sad lies
You never left – you only disappeared
You never left – you only disappeared from day one
Sever the skies
You told the lie – a perfect last night
You told the lie a perfect view from down in my grave
Sever the skies
Pig after pig

CALLAHAN

Bullet races
Small wonder
Gray matter spray
Breach open
Closing airwaves
A lovely evening – an overland view
Breathe in
Breathe in
Word erases
Small wonder
Hand slips away
Breach open closed connection
Wild animal stray
We dont fear the blazing sun
Through attrition is the battle won
Mark traces
All wonder
Spread with fortune few
Alarm sounding
Reaching outward
For hard fought grace
Bullet racing from the mouth of the blazing sun
Speeding – a powerful one – a beautiful one

KRAMER

Old north wind
Down style facing west again
Take away my burning night
Oh light
Oh shining light
Make right atrocity
Make whole complexity
Each cold word and deed
Adding stones to future fate
Each night in strange embrace
Making clear the hour is late
Blind leading sighted blind
Dead leading bruised and battered race
Clinging to implausibility
Flock to the much beleaguered shore
Where all these hurricanes are still craving ever more
The cleansing rain washes clean of all
Each cold word and deed
Adding stones to future fate
Each night in strange embrace
Making clear the hour is late
Locked down on shameful cross
Locked in cage of twisted thought
Still craving strange embrace
Such an effort — all for naught
Blind still leading sighted blind
Dead leading bruised and battered race
Where all these hurricanes are still craving ever more
The cleansing rain washes clean of all
Lost and defeated — left and beleaguered in shame

VEGA

How does it feel to burn?
How does it feel to lose?
I can't see – I'm unclean
I cant breathe – I wont leave
Did you even see the faded line?
Do you think ill make it back in time?
Am I the vision of your past unseen?
Do you remember when you left the scene?
You'll see my face before the grave
We'll meet again
Killing to win
Before the grave

VEGO

When you set it off
Nothing says I don't care
Like words from under breath
"I never said I did"
and you brought it back to our first night
but flames that burned are half as bright again
What's that mean? Another half truth told
To the wrong side of the door
Im gone And I won't be back again
I won't be back again
Light it up and burn it down – just walk away
just walk away
Round and bright
breeding black lines bathed in decadence
Waste and tear
scathing sunlight exposing evidence
watch with reverence at dawn
back and forth til hands are dead again
Held and watched – commendation still received
Born and bred – followed back to rivers edge
Lost and found – drinking deep but wondrous strong
A full grown man – who taught us right – we still know wrong
Held and watched – commendation still received
Born and bred – followed back to rivers edge
It's a foregone fate
And I'll stay away
But I'll reject your disgrace
See the smile on my face
See the smile on my face
And I'll destroy any trace
And I'll see the end of the race.

WADE GARRETT

Hey – scratching at your back door trying to get this dog a bone
Hey – sitting on your back porch tryin to work my way back home
I've been wallowing in my own filth hoping for an unmarked grave
I've been barking at the full moon struggling with this leash all day
Fall down and wonder if it's ever real –
fake smiles and hope you haven't spoiled the deal
Watching from a distance wondering – where the hell you'd go?
Stand on a thin line between the new and old
Under sea warmth – but on the surface cold
You hesitated when it comes to life and love
And confiscated when it comes to push and shove
Hey – remember when you'd take me out – parade me for the neighborhood
Still you leave me in the dog house for acting like a good dog should
You'd prefer to leave it all unsaid – don't deal well with reality
Yeah I've been there – so force a grin and blame your personality
Seems distant and cold to me
Never half what it appears to be
One mans gold can be another mans worn out soul
I used to stand the dark – you were the pinnacle – the goal
Now your spurious – an actor with a role
Bad water rising up
Overflowing from your golden cup
I used to get nervous at the sound of chains
I used to fear being left in the wind and the pouring rain
After all this time I find that i'm the one who's feared not the one whos left behind
When it's not just talk – the road you'll walk is unstoppable you'll find
Let one succeed instead of leaving two behind
Not giving up – never giving up
Still you make it tough – when you're controlling us
Burn the backyard down

(L-R) Jeff Martin – Vocals, Brian Fristoe – Guitar, Jesse Bartz – Drums, Skot Thompson – Bass

Wall Street 2007

Dumb Ass Fault
DUMB ASPHA~~ULT~~   8 aT oF 10. WAITED FOR TWO HOURS.

MANCHESTER NEW HAMPSHIRE (Mad Bob's)

   DUDES FROM THE BAND WHO'S NAME I CAN'T REMEMBER JUST SHOWED UP. THEY WERE LISTENING TO SCISSORFIGHT. THIS PARKING LOT DOESN'T SUCK. WELL PLACED PARKING RIGHT BEHIND THE STAGE DOOR. +1. SKATE PARKS AND BASEBALL STADIUMS FOR ENTERTAINMENT WHILE WE WAIT HERE FOR HOURS FOR NO FUCKING REASON. +1. ~~scribbled out~~ NOBODY SEEMS TO CARE THAT WE SMOKE WEED OR DRINK OUR OWN WHISKEY OUT HERE IN THE PARKING LOT +1 I FORGOT MY BANDANA. I'VE BEEN HERE FOR TWO HOURS. FUCK YOU.

<u>Northampton</u>, Mass. (The Elevens)   9/10   Arrived @ 3 pm

   Good parking lot. Great little town. Pizza shops (Multiple) within 2 blocks, Liquor store 1 block, and apparently weed is decriminalized here. I think we found a place to rent! Haha Great club set up easy load in. Beautiful weather today. Various couches for us to ~~s~~ soil. I think there are six bands on the bill tonight. Andy (Black Pyramid) set this ~~show~~ up. He works @ the grill/Bar next door. His band Dunge Bitd is also playing tonight. Overall great 1st impressions.

The phone all gangsta but I swear it's not even turned on. Sadly no bells on this trip yet!

6.2 Akron, OH — Annabells — arrive @ 3:30pm 7/10

We have spent many, many, many, many hours in this parking. Overall good lot. People give you some privacy. Quick and easy load in load-out. All the staff at Annabell's are extremely cool. Good spots to eat in the surrounding blocks. We beat BP in arriving early again. Having a great time on this tour with those guys/girl. We did Karaoke after our show. Jeff killed it with a George Michael song. I have slept in the van for the past 3 nights. I hate that fucking bunch. Plus I have only been able to sleep in 3 hour intervals. Had some good friends show up early to hang with us. Overall good parking lot + good friends = cookie.

6.3 Chicago, Ill. — Metal Shaker — arrive @ 6pm 9/10

THEY TRIED TO BEAT US HERE. THEY TRIED TO GET TO THE BOSS-ASS PARKING SPOT FIRST. BUT WE TOOK THE BACK WAY... THROUGH THE FUCKING GHETTO. GUESS WHO WON THE RACE? LO-PAN. GUESS WHO LOST? BACKWOODS PAYBACK. OUR SPOT IS THE DAMN FUCK SHIT. THEY EVEN HAD AN EZ PASS, BUT WE FLANKED 'EM.

Ford Econoline E150, Spring 2009

LO-PAN

ALSO Available from Aqualamb Artists

☐ **DESCENDER by Descender** (ALR 001)
6 song debut EP. Available formats: Digipak CD, digital download, streaming
90's Influenced Post-Hardcore. RIYL: Snapcase, Helmet, Quicksand

☐ **AND SO WE MARCHED by Descender** (ALR 002)
4 song EP. Available formats: Printed book, digital download, streaming
90's Influenced Post-Hardcore. RIYL: Snapcase, Helmet, Quicksand

☐ **TAKING DRUGS TO MAKE MUSIC TO SELL CARS TO** (ALR 003)
by Human Highlight Reel
4 song debut EP. Available formats: Vinyl record, printed book, digital download, streaming
Instrumental Post Rock. RIYL: Maserati, June of 44, Russian Circles

☐ **JUDGE by Vagina Panther** (ALR 004)
5 song EP. Available formats: Printed book, digital download, streaming
Heavy Female Fronted Garage Rock. RIYL: QOTSA, Cheeseburger, Fu Manchu, Stooges

☐ **BLACK BLACK BLACK by Black Black Black** (ALR 005)
12 song debut LP. Available formats: Vinyl record, printed book, digital download, streaming
Melodic Death Rock. RIYL: Akimbo, Torche, Lungfish, Black Flag

☐ **GODMAKER by Godmaker** (ALR 007)
4 song debut LP. Available formats: Vinyl record, printed book, digital download, streaming
Doomy Sludge Metal. RIYL: High on Fire, Red Fang, Mastodon, The Sword

☐ **THE SPACE MERCHANTS by The Space Merchants** (ALR 008)
8 song debut LP. Available formats: Printed book, digital download, streaming
Whiskey-soaked Space Rock. RIYL: Black Mountain, Black Angels, Dead Meadow, The Besnard Lakes

☐ **HIRAM-MAXIM by Hiram-Maxim** (ALR 009)
4 song debut LP. Available formats: Vinyl record, printed book, digital download, streaming
Noisy Experimental Doomgaze. RIYL: Swans, Suicide, Pink Floyd, Oxbow

☐ **ALTERED STATES OF DEATH AND GRACE by Black Black Black** (ALR 010)
10 song sophomore LP. Available formats: Vinyl record, printed book, digital download, streaming
Melodic Death Rock. RIYL: Akimbo, Torche, Lungfish, Black Flag

☐ **TRESPASSES by NATHANIEL SHANNON & THE VANISHING TWIN** (ALR 011)
Debut LP ian uninhibited glimpse into the murky corners of SHANNON's life-long fascination with the
psychology of lurid sounds and visual arts. Available formats: Printed book, digital download, streaming
Post-hardcore melodic rock. RIYL: Mark Lanegan, Angelo Badalemnti, Bruce Springsteen, Tom Waits.

☐ **FERA by HUSBANDRY** (ALR 012)
Debut full-length is a wild and sensual trip across nine unrelenting, masterfully crafted songs.
Available formats: Printed book, digital download, streaming Post-hardcore melodic rock. RIYL: Mars Volta,
Glassjaw, Refused, Deftones, and Faith No More.

☐ **MURDEREDMAN by MURDEREDMAN** (ALR 013)
8 song sophomore LP. Available formats: Vinyl record, printed book, digital download, streaming
Post-punk inspired noise rock. RIYL: Savages, Bauhaus, Boris, Killing Joke

All releases are available online at aqualamb.org

The music for *In Tensions*
can be downloaded
via the link below:

http://aqualamb.org/014

www.ingramcontent.com/pod-product-compliance
Lightning Source LLC
Chambersburg PA
CBHW051657040426
42446CB00009B/1189